BRITISH LORRIES
1900–1945

S. W. STEVENS-STRATTEN

AMBERLEY

This Morris design of 10 cwt van and truck proved popular with small concerns when introduced in 1938. The engine was offset to give room for the driver's legs.

First published 2019

Amberley Publishing
The Hill, Stroud
Gloucestershire, GL5 4EP

www.amberley-books.com

Copyright © S. W. Stevens-Stratten 2019

The right of S. W. Stevens-Stratten to be identified as the Author
of this work has been asserted in accordance with the
Copyrights, Designs and Patents Act 1988.

British Library Cataloguing in Publication Data.
A catalogue record for this book is available from the British Library.

ISBN 978 1 4456 9451 1 (print)
ISBN 978 1 4456 9452 8 (ebook)

Typeset in 10pt on 13pt Sabon.
Typesetting by Aura Technology and Software Services, India.
Printed in the UK.

Contents

A Pagefield mobile crane, similar to the ones used by the railway companies, loading a container on to a Pagefield chassis, c. 1929.

Introduction

'Natural progression' are two words widely used today to describe many different spheres of development, but in the field of mechanised transport the changes made in this century have had a significant effect on the lives of men and women in the greater part of the world. It is not only the motor car which has caused such dramatic changes

The interior of the cab of a Thornycroft forward control vehicle of 1938.

A 1938 Foden tractor produced in 1938 for a fairground operator which is still in use in the 1980s. (S. W. Stevens-Stratten)

to our lifestyle, but the progress and development made in buses and coaches, lorries and vans; even the farm tractor, for they have all played their part.

The transformation from the early days of commercial vehicles to the present time, despite restrictions and government legislation, is quite remarkable and the last 70 years have seen more changes than in most other forms of transport – not only the aesthetic or visual impact, but in terms of technical development.

Today a heavy lorry can undertake the journey from London to Bristol in 2½ hr, carrying a load of 32 tons reliably and safely, with the driver sitting in comfort protected from the weather, with heater, radio and cassette player in his cab. Such a journey 70 years ago would take as many days as it now takes hours, breakdowns were numerous, average speed was less than 12 mph, with the driver exposed to all the elements, sitting on a wooden plank, with virtually no springing or suspension on the vehicle and with poor road surfaces, a rough ride was inevitable. Incidentally, the load carried was unlikely to have exceeded 4/5 tons. One must not forget the horse, a noble and intelligent animal, but a story beyond the scope of this book.

The earlier book, compiled by my colleague and friend, the late Charles F. Klapper, was originally my idea. In compiling this present volume I have tried to portray a general selection of the vehicles seen on the road for the given period, but obviously it is not possible to mention or illustrate all the models produced, so I have tried to show some of the more popular vehicles, plus a few unusual ones. Naturally, the book confines itself to goods vehicles and is not intended to include examples of lorries which are bus-derived, or strange 'one-off' or specialised items.

Left: Hand cranking the tipping mechanism of a 1920 model T Ford which is now preserved. (S. W. Stevens-Stratten Collection)

Below: Daimler was not a commercial vehicle manufacturer in the true sense of the word. This light delivery van of c. 1910 is based on a car chassis. (S. W. Stevens-Stratten Collection)

I purposely have not included the small band of foreign makers who imported a few of their vehicles to this country and only partly assembled or serviced them here, for that is a subject in itself.

Unfortunately, many of the manufacturers featured in this book are no longer in business. In fact of the forty-eight makers mentioned, only nine are still in existence, and of this nine only two are still wholly British owned.

A few of the smaller British producers of commercial vehicles are included in the last chapter.

The text concerning each manufacturer is not intended to be a complete history, but more to give the salient points regarding the development of the company and its production.

I have tried to show vehicles which are actually in working trim, rather than manufacturers' preproduction photographs, which are often misleading. Some photographs of preserved vehicles have been included because the original is not available or has been seen in other publications.

Thanks must be given to the enthusiasts who have lovingly restored some of the old vehicles, spending a considerable amount of their time and money to give enjoyment to others. The Historic Commercial Vehicle Society (HCVS) was formed in 1956 to cater for the growing band of enthusiasts and is now the leading organisation in this field. There are many museums up and down the country where preserved vehicles are exhibited, and it would not be practical to list them all here, but mention must be made of the National Motor Museum at Beaulieu, Hampshire, and the British Commercial Vehicle Museum at Leyland, Lancashire. Both are well worth a visit.

I hope that this book will not only be useful as a work of reference for enthusiasts interested in old commercials, but it will also be a trip down memory lane for some of the older readers.

All photographs are from the Ian Allan Library unless otherwise credited.

S. W. Stevens-Stratten FRSA
Epsom, Surrey

AEC

The Associated Equipment Company (AEC) had its origins in Walthamstow as the servicing concern for the London Motor Omnibus Company (fleet name Vanguard), in 1906. A few years later Vanguard joined with others to form the London General Omnibus Co. This association with the old Vanguard firm was maintained as the telegraphic address for AEC remained 'Vangastow' until the end of its days.

On 13 June 1902, AEC was formed as a separate entity to build buses for London with the X-type and later the famous B-type coming into service. The first commercial vehicle was actually a lorry on the X-type chassis, but not until the First World War did AEC come into commercial vehicle production in earnest with a contract for 3 ton army lorries, designated the Y-type, of which more than 10,000 were built on a production line from 1916 to the end of the hostilities.

Variations on the Y-type were produced for the civilian market until 1923 when a 2½ ton chassis was introduced. This was the smallest vehicle AEC ever produced, all others having a minimum payload of 6 tons, but this model developed into the 204-type which remained in production until 1928.

The financial situation in the country was at a low ebb in 1926 and AEC entered into an agreement with Daimler for joint marketing under the name Associated Daimler. This only lasted for two years, after which both companies resumed their independent existence.

The fortunes of AEC rose rapidly and a brand new factory was built at Southall, with the move from Walthamstow completed in 1927. Another milestone was the appointment of G. J. Rackham as Chief Engineer and Designer in 1928 for his new ideas were incorporated in the production and the name of AEC became synonymous with quality and reliability.

From 1930 new models appeared with the now famous AEC inverted triangular badge, the range consisting of named models, all beginning with the letter M – Mammoth, Mercury, Majestic, etc. These models proved so successful that with a few exceptions they remained in production, with minor updated modifications until the end of the Second World War. AEC was also in the forefront of the production of the diesel engine, offering this as an alternative to the petrol engine in the mid-1930s.

During the Second World War, the company had an impressive record with the manufacture of Matador and Marshal vehicles for the services, as well as tanks and special components, also undertaking many experimental projects on behalf of the government.

In 1916 the standard Y type subsidy 3 ton lorry was introduced and a year later an improved model, the YA type, was made. Over 10,000 of these vehicles were supplied to the War Department by 1919. A 30 hp engine was fitted. Many of these vehicles were purchased by civilian operators after the war, and the basically similar YB and YC types continued in production until 1921.

Still on solid tyres in 1930, although by this time pneumatics could be fitted, this Mammoth 7/8 ton lorry had a six-cylinder overhead valve engine developing 110 bhp (45 hp on RAC rating) with a wheelbase of 16ft 7in.

A normal control Mercury canvas covered truck of 1928–29, for 4 ton payloads. The wheelbase is 14ft and overall length 21ft 7in. The petrol tank was under the driver's seat.

One of 10 Mercury (model 640) 3½ ton tankers which were supplied in 1930 to the Anglo American Oil Co. A four-cylinder petrol engine developed 65 bhp at 2,000 rpm. The wheelbase was 14ft and the total length was 20ft 5in.

The Matador 5 ton chassis was introduced in 1932, and had many similarities with the Mercury, but this particular vehicle was fitted with an AEC/Ricardo oil engine.

The normal control Majestic of 1930 (model 666) was for 6 ton payloads and from 1931 was only available on pneumatic tyres, but there was the option of a petrol or diesel engine.

The Monarch Mk II (model 637) of 1933 was an updated version of the original type of the same name introduced three years earlier as model 641. The payload was increased to 7½ tons and alternative petrol or oil engines were offered. This model remained in production until 1935.

This 1934 Mammoth Major eight-wheeled tank lorry was purchased new by a Liverpool concern and is now preserved by the Science Museum. The Mammoth Major Mk II was introduced in 1935 for 15 ton loads and remained in production until 1948, when the Mk III appeared, although it was basically similar. (S. W. Stevens-Stratten)

2

Albion

The Albion Motor Company was founded by T. Blackwood-Murray and N. O. Fulton (late of Arrol-Johnson), at Bathgate in Scotland in 1901.

In that year it manufactured a tiller-steered, two-cylinder, 8 hp dogcart. A year later the firm put a van body to a somewhat similar vehicle to carry 10 cwt loads (later the engine size was increased to 10 hp). This was the beginning of a highly successful company, for in 1904 Albion moved to a large factory at Scotstoun.

Many different models were made in their first decade, the most successful being the A10 model which appeared in 1910 for 3/4 ton loads using a four-cylinder, 32 hp engine. Like most Albions, the success lay in the simplicity of the original design, for example a patented ignition system devised by W. Blackwood-Murray, which continued from the early days until 1923. The A10 model made Albion well known for its reliability and it lasted in production for 16 years, and by the end of the war in 1918, nearly 6,000 had been supplied to the services.

In the 1920s Albion adopted the slogan 'Sure as the Sunrise' and the radiators had the setting sun motif with the name Albion in the distinctive lettering. During the 1920s and 1930s the firm prospered and many new models were introduced ranging from 30 cwt to 15 ton. Albion was early in the field with the forward control layout, which it called 'cab-over' types. Apart from its bus chassis, Albion was late in giving names to its range of vehicles, and used an unwieldy combination of letters and figures to denote the chassis model.

In 1935 Albion acquired the factory used to produce the Halley vehicles, which had ceased manufacture, and the building was used as a service depot, also as a packing plant for spares and export CKD vehicles.

Albion also made the chassis for a number of Merryweather fire appliances, most of which were fitted with Albion engines.

In the Second World War, Albion made many vehicles for the services including some large tractive units for tank transporters and recovery work.

A 1907 model A3 15 cwt van with a 16 hp engine. This model was in production from 1904 to 1915.

The longest production record is for the model T Ford, but this surely must come second. The Albion model A10 3-ton chassis was made from 1910–1926. Powered by a four-cylinder 32 hp engine, it had a wheelbase of 13ft 1in, but in 1920 it was available with an extended wheelbase of 14ft 5in.

A 2½ ton platform lorry of 1932. The shape of the cab is typical of many vehicles of the 1920s.

Albion was in the forefront for the forward control (or cab-over-engine) configuration, and this 5 ton overtype van from 1931 is a typical example. It was owned by a well-known firm of transport contractors.

A 3 ton long-wheelbase, 14ft platform lorry. It was one of two used to carry casks of tobacco leaf from a bonded warehouse to a factory four miles away.

In 1936 Albion produced a popular chassis, designated B119, which was fitted with a four-cylinder petrol engine of 19.6 hp. The wheelbase was 9ft 9in, and this example had a Strachans-built body with internal measurements of 13ft 6in length by 6ft 3in height.

Albion chassis were popular for the exotic coachwork of the decade. This 1935 example on a 30/40 cwt chassis is by Holland Coachcraft, a firm which made similar bodies for Collars Ltd.

A 10-ton six-wheeler fitted with an Albion six-cylinder direct injection oil engine. It was supplied to a Perth haulage contractor at the beginning of the Second World War. It has an unladen weight of 5 ton, 12 cwt.

3

Armstrong-Saurer

Saurer vehicles were produced in Switzerland and had an enviable reputation for their strength and reliability. As far back as 1907 Pickfords had imported a number, and ordered more in the 1920s. In 1930 the Saurer organisation decided that its vehicles should be made in the UK under licence, and thus Armstrong Whitworth began the manufacture at its Scotswood-on-Tyne works. The first Armstrong-Saurer, as the English models were named, was shown at the Commercial Motor Show in 1931. Originally it had been intended that all the complete vehicles would be built on Tyneside, but with production also taking place near Paris, some parts were imported – a similar practice being perfected by Ford some four decades later.

The Armstrong-Saurer vehicles proved successful and popular with all who were engaged in the heavy haulage business, and when eventually replaced, many ended their days with fairground operators. The vehicles had a rugged look about them, which indeed was indicative of the whole breed. Saurer was an early champion of the oil engine, with which its lorries were all fitted, also air-brakes and overdrive – great advances for the early 1930s.

All the models were given names such as the Active, 7 ton rigid four-wheeler; the Dynamic, 9 and 10 ton six-wheeler, the Samson, 15-ton rigid eight, etc. Production ceased in 1937, and unfortunately, as far as we know, only one has been preserved.

The Durable 6/7-ton chassis was supplied with the six-cylinder 110 bhp oil engine. This vehicle with an insulated van body for the carriage of meat was the fifth repeat order from Fairclough Bros in 1933.

A 7-ton Dominant six-wheeler in use by a firm known for road surfaces. The Dominant remained in production from 1932–34 and the price of the chassis was £1,750.

The Effective 6/7 tonner (12/14 tons with trailer) was produced from 1934 until manufacture ceased. It was also fitted with the six-cylinder 110 bhp engine of 111 mm bore by 150 mm stroke.

4

Atkinson

The name of Atkinson, in the field of road transport, goes back to 1907, when Edward Atkinson began to service and repair steam wagons and became an agent for Alley & McLellan, the originators of the Sentinel steamcars.

The first steam wagon to carry the Atkinson name was built in 1916, a conventional four-wheeler for a 6-ton payload, and production reached three vehicles a week in the early 1920s.

Despite its production of steamers, the firm floundered financially in the depression of the late 1920s, but continued to undertake the construction of trailers and the servicing and repair of vehicles.

The company was reconstituted as Atkinson Lorries Ltd in 1933 under the management of W. G. Allen of Nightingale Garage of Clapham (South London). A conventional forward control 6-ton four-wheel vehicle was produced using the Gardner diesel engine as the power unit. This was followed by a six-wheeler using the same cab and in 1937 an eight-wheeled rigid for 15-ton payloads. From then on the company never looked back and although producing only a few vehicles they were of high quality and began to win favourable comments from their operators.

Wartime contracts enhanced Atkinson's position, particularly on the financial side, for in 1940 it was awarded a Ministry of Supply contract for sixty six-wheel chassis fitted with Gardner 6LW engines, followed a year later by an order for 100 similar chassis, but this time fitted with the AEC 7.7 litre engine, and finally another 100 similarly engined chassis.

After the Second World War, Atkinson launched a new range of four-, six- and eight-wheeled vehicles, all employing Gardner engines.

This Atkinson Colonial steam lorry was built in 1918. It is believed to be the only one in preservation and was brought back from Australia. The three-way tipping body carries a 6-ton load.

A 9½/10-ton 'Chinese' six-wheeler which was produced in 1937. The cab is standard for all Atkinson models of this era.

An eight-wheeled 15 tonner of 1938 engaged on night trunk routes.

5

Austin

The name Austin is usually associated with cars and the Austin Seven or 'Chummy' in particular. The first cars were produced in 1908 and shortly afterwards a van body was fitted to one of these early models. The first real commercial vehicle was a 3 ton lorry produced in 1913, and this was perhaps unique as it had a forward control layout – the engine being on and slightly below the cab floor, with the radiator behind the four-cylinder 29 hp engine. There was also divided drive, two prop shafts each driving a bevel connected to the stub rear axles.

The production of commercial vehicles never achieved prominence and finished in 1922; the years following only seeing light vans based on car chassis with similar engines. Ambulances were also car-derived and based on the Austin 18 or 20 saloon models.

The company seriously entered the commercial vehicle market again in 1938 when it developed a range of lorries and vans ranging from 30 cwt to 5-ton. Outwardly the range resembled their rivals Bedford, the difference being noticeable in the radiator – in fact the new range became known as the Birmingham Bedfords.

During the Second World War, Austin made many vehicles for the services, including the 2/3-ton K2 chassis for army ambulances and the ATVs (auxiliary towing vehicles) for the fire services; the K3 general service 3 tonner; the K5 four-wheel drive 3 tonners (known as 'Screamers' due to the noise from the gearbox and transmission); and the K6 and 6x4-type used as RAF bowsers (aircraft refuellers).

An Austin 10/12 cwt van which is based on the Austin Twenty car chassis. This type of vehicle was built from 1924 onwards. From the end of 1929 two wheelbases were offered – 10ft 10in or 11 ft 4in – and in 1932 synchromesh gearboxes were introduced.

One of the many ambulances which were built on the Austin Twenty chassis. This example dates from 1936.

Again using a car chassis, this is the 1937 version of the 12 hp van.

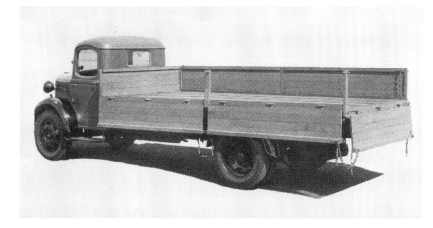

The immediate pre-war Austin 5 ton chassis showing the rear of the cab and inside of the wooden-planked lorry.

The handsome lines of the radiator, bonnet and cab of the K series of commercial vehicles which appeared in 1939. This is a well restored K2 truck, a 2/3 tonner using a six-cylinder petrol engine of 26.8 hp. Lockheed hydraulic brakes operated on all wheels. (S. W. Stevens-Stratten)

The Austin 5 ton chassis carrying a petrol tank body.

Again, pleasing lines for the design of this 30 cwt box van supplied to Liverpool Corporation for distributing milk to hospitals in the area.

6

Bean

Bean Cars Ltd, with its works at Waddams Pool, Tipton, Dudley, Worcestershire, was an offshoot of A. Harper & Sons Ltd which was founded in 1901 and was well established as a component manufacturer for the motor vehicle industry. In 1919 the company decided to produce complete motor cars itself, and a few years later made its first commercial vehicle.

In 1925, Bean produced a 25 cwt lorry with a 13.9 hp engine selling at a competitive price and this was replaced two years later by an updated version. However, at this time the company had run into financial difficulties and the steel suppliers, Hadfield, had taken control of the company, although allowing Bean to keep its separate identity.

The 'Empire' chassis for 50 cwt loads was produced and then in 1929 a 30 cwt vehicle, using a 46 bhp Hadfield engine from one of the Bean car range was offered for only £325. Bean decided that due to fierce competition in the car market it would concentrate solely on commercial vehicle production, and in 1931 produced the New Era 20–25 cwt chassis.

Competition in this market was equally fierce and Bean reduced the price of its products over the years in an effort to beat the larger firms such as Ford, Morris and Dodge, but in the end the profit margin became negligible and the company went into liquidation in 1931. Fortunately, the company was reformed and continued to supply components to the motor industry.

A 4 ton forward control flat platform lorry of 1930.

In 1931 Bean introduced the 20/25 cwt New Era chassis, seen here as a delivery van.

A fleet of New Era vans supplied to the Kensington catering firm of Slaters in 1931.

7

Beardmore

William Beardmore & Co. Ltd are better known as the manufacturer of the taxicabs which it first produced in 1919, and these were so successful that the company carried out some market research and in 1923 brought out an improved model which, again, was highly popular. The taxicabs were manufactured in Paisley, Scotland and retailed through Beardmore's own taxicab company in London.

In 1930 the company acquired the patents for the production of the French Chenard-Walcker tractor, which via the coupling allowed part of the trailer weight to be taken on the tractor which, of course, increased the adhesion. The vehicles were produced at Clapham in South London.

Beardmore produced the Anaconda, a 15 ton multi-wheeler; the Python for 10/15 ton loads; and the Cobra which was a 10 ton tractor unit. All used Meadows engines.

In 1932, Beardmore sold this part of its business to a syndicate calling itself Multiwheelers, which became an independent company. The engines in the vehicles were usually AEC or Gardner from this time onwards. Multiwheelers ceased production in 1937.

A recently restored Beardmore articulated unit in 1984. (S. W. Stevens-Stratten Collection)

8

Bedford (and Chevrolet)

Chevrolet vehicles had been imported from the USA and were even assembled at Hendon in the late 1920s. The last of these models were the LQ and LT trucks for 30 cwt payloads, both using a six-cylinder engine of 26.6 hp, with a 'splash' lubrication system, and known as the 'cast iron wonder'. The firm moved to Luton, and as its parent company, General Motors, wished to improve the sales and expand the Chevrolet range, it was placed under the wing of General Motors' car producer, Vauxhall Motors.

In 1931 the range was completely redesigned and produced under the name Bedford. Success was immediate, for the range proved to be fast and reliable which won it popularity with all branches of the road haulage industry. The Bedford slogan 'You See Them Everywhere' was absolutely true.

Their first models used the same cab as the Chevrolet, but there the difference ended. The first model (the WHG) was a 2 tonner (10ft 11in wheelbase), the WLG was a 2 tonner (13ft 1in wheelbase), and the WS was for 30 cwt loads and a wheelbase of 10ft 11in. All three used the Bedford six-cylinder 26.3 hp petrol engine, and all remained in production until 1939 when the new range was announced. In 1934 the model BYC 12 cwt van was introduced which proved to be the best light delivery van in its class. In the same year the WTL model for tippers made an appearance. All these vehicles had flat fronted radiators.

In 1939, Bedford announced a completely new range with attractive curved radiator grilles and more curved cab outlines. The K models were for 30–40 cwt payloads, with standard wheelbase of 10ft, using a six-cylinder 27.3 hp petrol engine. The designations were KZ for chassis only; KC for chassis and cab; KD for a dropside lorry and KV for a van.

The M series was for 2–3-ton loads with 10ft or 11ft 11in wheelbase, the designations being as for the K series, except MST which was the shorter wheelbase model as a tipper.

The O series was for 3/4 ton and 5 ton loads, with two alternative wheelbases, but apart from chassis and cab the range was for lorries or tippers. The shorter wheelbase (9ft 3in) was also available as a prime mover for articulated vehicles.

During the Second World War Bedford made many different kinds of vehicles for the Services, a total of 250,000, among them the famous QL range of forward control four-wheel drive vehicles.

One of the first 2 ton Bedfords of 1931 — note the preface 'British' on the bonnet side. This long wheelbase version, complete with dropside body cost £260!

This breakdown truck complete with crane and searchlight was new in 1934 to the London County Council Motor Vehicle Repair Depot.

An early 2 ton chassis was used by Curtis for mounting the three-horse box shown here unloading at a hunt meeting.

A 3 ton short wheelbase chassis is used for this hydraulic end tipper with the pump driven directly from the gearbox take-off. It is powered by the six-cylinder overhead valve 27 hp engine, which had a long production run. The body has a steel-lined floor and top-hinged tailboard. The price in 1937 was £327.

The good-looking design of this 30 cwt delivery van is evident in this side view, as is the generous space for signwriting or advertising.

The 30 cwt van was very popular before the Second World War, and this is an example on contract hire to Cadbury-Fry.

HM Queen Elizabeth, now the Queen Mother, inspects a convoy of wartime Bedford vans donated by the American Committee for Air Raid Relief.

A 5 ton Bedford chassis is used for this 900-gal Thompson tank body which transported sodium sulphate for the Crow Carrying Co. in 1941.

9

Bristol

The Bristol Tramways & Carriage Co. Ltd was a bus operator which manufactured its own passenger carrying vehicles from 1908. It was not unnatural that the firm should produce a few commercial vehicles, the first two being exhibited at the Royal Agricultural Show in Bristol in 1913. These were a brewers' dray and a dairy produce wagon.

Eighteen vehicles were supplied to the RNAS between July 1914 and January 1915. The next production was an experimental W type lorry in 1915, and postwar production was a development of this in 1920 which was designated as the 4 ton model. A total of 649 of this type of chassis was produced, at least 132 being filled with commercial bodywork, mainly tankers and lorries. Production of this type finished in 1931.

A 2 ton forward control model was introduced in 1923 and a total of 267 was built. Initially seventy-three were fitted with commercial bodywork mainly for petrol distribution.

In 1932 Bristol became part of the Thomas Tilling Croup and all commercial production ceased in favour of passenger chassis.

The firm, renamed Bristol Commercial Vehicles, re-entered the goods vehicle field in 1953, which is outside the period covered by this volume.

This 1920 Bristol dropside lorry was exhibited at the 1920 Commercial Motor Show and was used by Bristol Tramways from 1923–31 when it was sold to a showman who used it until the early 1950s. It has since been fully restored and is seen here at the Wheels of Yesterday Rally in Battersea Park in 1986. (S. W. Stevens-Stratten)

10

Caledon

Scottish Commercial Cars Ltd of Duke Street, Glasgow was a distributor for Commer vehicles, but in 1914 found that these vehicles were unavailable for the civilian market. Realising that its main activity would suffer, the company decided to set up its own manufacturing concern, using Dorman engines and Dux gearboxes (from France).

The first vehicle was produced in 1915 and a range of 3, 3½ and 4 ton chassis followed. The vehicles were basic and suffered from back axle problems among other malfunctions. At the end of the First World War some 380 had been built, of which seventy-six were supplied to the Ministry of Munitions, after having been rejected earlier.

After the war the firm, now named Caledon Motors, was to produce a range from 30 cwt to 7 ton, also manufacturing its own engines. Unfortunately the flood of cheap and good ex-WD lorries coming on the market decreased potential sales to such an extent that the firm ran into financial difficulties as early as 1922, but it struggled on until 1926, when it was acquired by Garretts.

A 1919 Caledon model E 4 ton lorry, which remained in production until 1926. Powered by a four-cylinder (120 mm by 140 mm) petrol engine, the maximum speed was 12 mph at 5 mpg. The wheelbase was 14ft 3in. (S. W. Stevens-Stratten)

Commer

Commercial Cars Ltd was formed in 1905 and the title immediately shortened to Commer. The early models were designated CC and featured the Lindley epicyclic preselector gearbox, the gear lever unusually mounted on the steering column. Even its early models ranged from 1 ton to 6 ton which was quite a heavy vehicle for those days, and they were exported to many countries including the USA.

During the First World War, Commer produced over 3,000 model RC 4 ton lorries. Soon after hostilities ended there were so many ex-WD vehicles coming on the market that Commer, like other manufacturers, was not selling new vehicles and this, plus the general depression of the mid-1920s led the company into financial difficulties.

Commer was taken over by Humber Cars in 1926. Humber renamed its Centaur Co. (founded in 1911) as Commer Cars Ltd. Hence the use of the name Centaur (and Raider) for some of the Commer range in the 1930s.

The Rootes Group took over the Humber/Hillman/Commer companies in 1928, and from then onwards Commer was on a sound financial footing. Some smaller vehicles were introduced and soon a 10 cwt van appeared based on the Hillman Minx car. The Rootes Group also acquired Karrier Motors in 1934; therefore in later years there was a certain amount of standardisation between the two makes. In 1935 Commer introduced its successful N range of normal and forward control for vans and lorries up to 5 ton.

Just prior to the outbreak of the Second World War in 1939, the Superpoise (Q model) range was announced with five good-looking vehicles from 30 cwt to 6 tons with short bonnets. The engine protruded into the cab, but they proved popular with a wide variety of operators.

During the Second World War, Commer produced over 20,000 vehicles for the fighting forces including Q4 (Superpoise) 4–5-ton lorries (army rating 3 ton), and tractive units for the 60ft long Queen Mary trailers used by the RAF for carrying aircraft fuselage.

A 1908 Commer loaded with apples in a Kentish orchard at the start of a journey to London.

A good load is being carried on this G2 model 2/2½ ton lorry which is powered by a six-cylinder engine.

A model G4 lorry built in 1931 for a 4 ton payload, supplied to the Runcorn & Widnes Industrial Co-operative Society Ltd. A year later this model was redesignated GL4, being of lighter construction and available as normal or forward control versions.

The 1½ ton Raider model was introduced in 1932 with a six-cylinder side valve engine of 22.6 hp. The wheelbase was 10ft 6in. The model remained in action until 1935.

In the same year the Centaur model was announced for 2 ton loads. The vehicle seen here is in Smithfield Market, Birmingham.

The 6/8 cwt van of 1933 is based on the Hillman Minx car. The chassis cost £125, or the complete van £150.

A forward control version of the Centaur 2 tonner fitted with a loose tilt body and supplied new in 1934.

In 1935, Commer introduced the N series of vehicles ranging from 8 cwt to 5 tons. Here is a model N2 van with attractive signwriting.

The Commer Superpoise range succeeded the N series in 1939. The name Superpoise was inspired by the well balanced loading conditions of the range, which were offered with petrol or diesel engines, forward or normal control, and with a wide variety of wheelbases. Shown here is a 4/5 ton lorry. The radiator, bonnet and cab was similar for most of the range.

12

Dennis

John Dennis started his business career building cycles in 1885, his younger brother, Raymond, soon joining the expanding concern. The next step was his Speed King motorcycles, and thus to motor cars. Dennis Brothers Ltd produced its first commercial vehicle in 1904 which was a 15 cwt van with a four-cylinder 12 hp engine. This vehicle probably had the patented Dennis worm gear rear axle, which, of course, dispensed with the chain drive used on practically all other vehicles. The first Dennis fire engine was built in 1908 for Bradford and Dennis have been famous for their various fire appliances ever since.

Dennis produced many different commercial vehicles using the White & Poppe four-cylinder T-head 40 hp engine, and in 1913 produced its Model A subsidy 3½ ton lorry (3 ton army rating). Approximately 7,000 were produced.

In 1919 Dennis purchased White & Poppe Ltd which had supplied it and other manufacturers with engines. In the 1920s Dennis produced a large number of lighter chassis of 30 cwt, 2 ton and 3 ton capacity which were fitted with van and lorry bodies. Dennis also produced 6 tonners, forward control models being introduced in 1927, and shortly afterwards the M type 12 ton six-wheeler appeared, but this was not a success as only thirty-six had been sold by the time the model was taken out of their range in 1936. In 1934 the firm produced its own Dennis diesel engine.

One of the successes was the 40/45 cwt chassis (called Ace for buses), which had the engine ahead of the front axle, giving a 'snout' effect and thus earning the nickname of 'Flying Pig'. A forward control version with the engine in the cab was also produced. In 1937 the Max 12 ton six-wheel chassis was produced, also a 5 ton four-wheeler, which after the Second World War was given the name Pax.

Dennis had many contracts with municipal authorities and the range of refuse collectors, gully emptiers, street washers, etc. were very popular. Their fire appliances were in a class of their own, the only other rival of any size being Leyland.

During the Second World War Dennis produced vehicles for the government and essential civilian operators, as well as hundreds of trailer pumps for the fire services and undertook much subcontracted work including the assembly of Churchill tanks and the manufacture of gearboxes.

Introduced in 1926, the 4 ton Dennis is a normal control (13ft 1½in or 14ft 1½in wheelbase) lorry powered by a Dennis four-cylinder petrol engine of 30 hp. The vehicle shown here is a 1927 model beautifully preserved and often seen at rallies. (Stevens-Stratten Collection)

This 1931 3½ ton Luton type pantechnicon has a body built by Clement, Butler & Cross.

A typical Dennis normal control 3 tonner of the early 1930s. The body has a capacity of 1,000 cu ft.

Dennis vehicles were always in favour with municipal authorities. This is one of two lorries supplied to the County Borough of East Ham to carry 3 tons of household refuse.

This 7 ton lorry was fitted with a Gardner six-cylinder diesel engine which due to its length necessitated a longer bonnet, giving a 'Bulldog' look to the vehicle. Note the single rear wheels on the third axle.

In 1935 the Dennis Ace was introduced to meet the competition from the mass production market in the 2/2½ ton range. This is a 750 gal multipurpose gully emptier, but this side view aptly describes the nickname given to the normal control Ace as the 'Flying Pig'!

The forward control version of the Ace proved popular as it enabled the maximum space for a load within the minimum length of vehicle, also it was highly manoeuvrable. This was a 40/45 cwt model used by a well-known parcels carrier.

At the end of 1935 a completely new Light Four 4 tonner made an appearance using an elongated Ace radiator shell.

From its earliest days Dennis has always been one of the premier manufacturers of fire appliances. This is a Dennis Big Four featuring a six-cylinder petrol engine and a 800 gal/min pump. It has transverse seating for the crew, which is safer than the Braidwood style where men sat facing outwards and could be flung off if the driver was over zealous in taking a corner! This is a 1935 machine with steel escape.

13

Dodge

The Dodge Brothers, John and Horace, produced the first motor car bearing their name in the USA in 1918, shortly afterwards producing some light commercial vehicles. These were imported into the UK, among the first being a 15 cwt delivery van, which was popular with newspaper distributors and others as it was a fast vehicle.

The range was distributed by agents, but in 1923 Dodge Bros (GB) Ltd was formed and a small factory purchased in Stevenage Road, Fulham. Three years later this moved to larger premises near Park Royal, London NW10. The vehicles produced at this time consisted of a 15 cwt van, a 1 ton chassis, shortly joined by a 1½ ton chassis, but all these were marketed with the Graham badge, one of the Dodge subsidiaries.

In 1928, the Dodge Bros concern was purchased by the Chrysler Corporation and the UK Dodge production moved to the Chrysler factory at Kew.

In 1933 the first British produced Dodge vehicles appeared, a 30 cwt and 2 ton and 4 ton chassis, but still with the American built engine. From the mid-1930s the Dodge vehicles became a familiar sight on the British roads, particularly the 6 ton tipper lorry, which was favoured by many contractors and sand and gravel merchants. The first truly all-British Dodge was produced in 1938 when it was fitted with a Perkins diesel engine. During the war the Kew factory was given over to the manufacture of components for aircraft production including the Halifax bombers.

A 30 cwt chassis with van body by Wilsons (Kingston) Ltd with the whole of the side panelling in stainless steel.

One of the early Graham Bros standard 15 cwt delivery vans of 1928, fitted with a 24 hp four-cylinder engine at a cost of £250 complete.

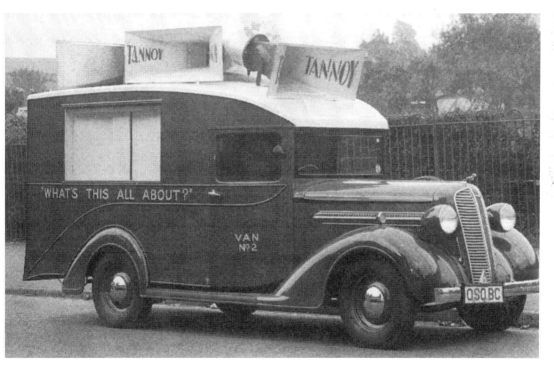

How appearances have changed in the space of ten years! This is a 1937 Dodge 15 cwt van used for public address work. It was used by a local rag and bone man to announce his presence.

A 1935 Dodge 3 ton chassis
with a three-compartment
1,500 gal steel tank body.

A 1939 Dodge 6 ton
chassis fitted with a
tank body.

A 1938 Dodge 6 ton truck
carrying a car of the same
make and year, seen outside
the works at Kew.

14

ERF

This is a comparative newcomer to commercial vehicle production, although the initials ERF stand for Edwin Richard Foden, a member of the family who had been in the vehicle manufacturing business since 1888. A disagreement regarding the building of diesel engined lorries instead of the steam vehicles for which Foden was famous, resulted in Edwin starting his own company in 1933. In the first year fourteen four-wheel, 6 ton lorries with Gardner 4LW, 65 bhp engines were produced. Various wheelbase options were offered, but all had four-speed crash gearboxes, a single-plate clutch and overhead worm rear axle. A year later a five-speed gearbox was optional.

A year after production commenced, the firm moved into the Sun Works at Sandbach (Cheshire), for the company soon found many customers as its products proved to be rugged and reliable. A 7 ton version of the original model but fitted with a Gardner 5LW engine quickly appeared and in 1935 a 5 ton four-wheeler, again with three different wheelbases (8ft 5in, 11ft 2in, or 12ft 5in) was available. All these models were of forward control layout and all were in production until the end of the war. A six-wheeler was offered in 1934 and the first of the ERF rigid eights appeared in 1936.

This ERF four-wheel 6 tonner was supplied to Bulmers Cider and is a good example of the early models.

The standard ERF forward control four-wheeled 6 tonner.

15

FWD

Four Wheel Drive of Milwaukee, USA, was formed in 1904, but was not known in this country until the First World War when the US Army used FWD products in France. The vehicles were made with a track width of 4ft 8½in so they could quickly be used on a standard gauge railway line by merely changing the wheels.

After the First World War many were offered by the government to the general public and were used by hauliers, forestry contractors and showmen who found the four-wheel drive extremely effective in obtaining traction on rough and muddy ground.

An English subsidiary was set up at Slough in 1921, first converting the original US Army models, and then producing lorries for general transport. In 1926, the British FWD, or Quad as it was sometimes known was produced with a larger 70 bhp engine. Most of the models had a high cab sited over the engine.

A subsidiary company, Hardy Rail Motors, was formed for rail traction, but both companies found insufficient sales for such specialist vehicles and AEC took a controlling interest in the company in 1932. Some of the rail designs were incorporated in the AEC railcars which were produced shortly afterwards.

After the agreement with AEC, the FWD was redesigned to utilise more standard AEC components, and to avoid confusion with the American machines, the British vehicles were marketed under the name Hardy. Production seems to have ceased about 1936. FWDs were again imported into this country during the Second World War, but were a vastly different looking vehicle.

A FWD chassis supplied to Norway and fitted with a Gorman centrifugal pump on the rear and searchlight mounted on a tank behind the driver's seat. This illustrates the height of the driving position.

A standard 4 ton chassis fitted with a three-way hydraulic tipping body on pneumatic tyres.

A tipper with a later type of cab but on solid tyres.

16

Foden

Foden began making steam traction engines as far back as 1882, with regular production a couple of years later. The first Foden steam lorry was produced in 1900, and from that time the Foden name became synonymous with such vehicles, which continued to be manufactured until 1932.

In 1902 the steam lorry was a regular production at the Elworth Works, Sandbach, which was taken over from Plant & Hancock. The standard machines were overtype models, which had the cylinders and engine mounted on top of the boiler, with the flywheels just below the steering handle; the steersman half standing in a fairing (or 'scuttle') on the near-side. These wagons had a load capacity of 5 tons and a wheelbase of 14ft 10in. They remained in production until 1923.

In 1920 an improved overtype made its appearance, again for a 6 ton payload, but with many improvements – both crew members now being accommodated in the open type cab. Boiler pressure was 200 lb/sq in for the compound engine with steam jacketed cylinders of 4¼in (high pressure) and 7in (low pressure), both having a 7in stroke. Three wheelbases were available – 10ft 6in for tractors; 13ft 10in for a tipper; and 14ft 9in for the standard chassis.

The crippling taxation and other restrictions imposed on steam-driven vehicles, plus the increasing efficiency of the petrol and diesel engines, caused the death of the steam lorry, so, reluctantly, Foden turned its attention to diesel lorries. The first of the new production – a 6 ton lorry – was supplied in July 1931, and the last steam vehicle was produced in 1933.

The first diesel vehicle had a Gardner engine fitted and thus started a long association between the two companies. All Foden models were of the forward control layout and the range prior to the Second World War was from 6 ton rigid four-wheelers to 15 ton eight-wheelers, many of the models having the distinctive curved-fronted cab. The coding for the vehicles denoted engine type and payload – DG5/15 would be a DG model fitted with a Gardner 5LW engine to carry a 15 ton load. Foden also made a number of diesel powered timber tractors.

During the war Foden produced 1,750 vehicles for the War Department, 770 Crusader and Centaur tanks and over 7½ million 20mm shells.

An early Foden steam wagon of 1910 with steel wheels, tyres and brake blocks. Note the maximum speed on the chassis frame!

The 5 ton Foden steamer was introduced in 1902 and continued in production until 1923. This beautifully-restored example dates from 1916. (Stevens-Stratten Collection)

This C type was built in 1922 and has attended many rallies since it was preserved. Note the front axle suspension. (Stevens-Stratten Collection)

One of the last Foden steam lorries was this 1931 Speed-12 undertype 10/12 ton tipper built to carry farm manure and chemicals. The water supply is in the tank behind the cab.

The first diesel lorry produced by Fodens – the R type – in 1931. Fitted with a Gardner 5L2 oil engine, it carried a 6 ton load. (Stevens-Stratten Collection)

By 1933 Fodens had a production line for the 4/6 ton lorry shown here.

A type DG5/7½ lorry with a body length of 16ft. The first figure of the model type was the number of cylinders (i.e. 5LW), the second figure was the payload in tons.

A 10 ton six-wheeler for 12-ton loads.

This 1937 example represents the ultimate in design for a 15 ton eight-wheeler.

17

Ford

Henry Ford is reputed to have said that his customers could have any colour for their vehicle, as long as it was black! The American-built vehicles were imported from 1904, and reached such numbers that an assembly plant was set up at Trafford Park, Manchester in 1911. In 1911 the famous Model T with a load capacity of 7 cwt was available, and shortly afterwards the updated and 'stretched' Model TT for 1 ton loads was made. The Model T continued in production until 1927 – a period of sixteen years.

The Model A for 15 cwt loads and the AA and AAF for 20–30 cwt were in production from 1928-1933, both models using the four-cylinder, 40 bhp engine and four-speed gearbox. Wire wheels were later replaced by a disc type.

The works at Dagenham commenced production in 1931 when the B (15–25 cwt) and the BB and BBF (2 ton) were made at first using the same engine, although shortly afterwards a 65 bhp V8 engine was introduced, but this had a problem with high oil consumption.

From 1935 models were called 'Fordson' and semi-forward control was available on certain models, the range being from 2 ton to 5 ton, fitted with a four-cylinder 24 hp engine or the 30 hp V8 engine. The 5 cwt van was based on the 8 hp car, using some of the same body components. Two interesting models were the Surrey and Sussex six-wheelers, the latter having a double drive rear axle.

The 7V series were introduced from 1937 for payloads of 2 ton to 5 ton with a choice of different wheelbases. Perkins diesel engines could also be fitted as an optional extra. Hydraulic brakes became standard on all models from 1939 and from March of that year all the Dagenham-built vehicles were named Thames.

During the Second World War, Ford produced a large number of the 7V series for the government, some being used as the basis for a Home Office fire appliance. Army vehicles included the type WOT 15 cwt truck, and the 3 ton 4x4 general service lorry.

A 1923 model T Ford flat truck, now preserved and seen at a rally. (Stevens-Stratten Collection)

In 1932 the Woolwich dealers for Ford, Herwin Canny & Co, supplied ten Ford AAF models to a firm of road haulage contractors.

Another Ford model A with bodywork for carrying livestock or market garden produce.

This stylish van is a Fordson 15 cwt of 1936.

This pre-war 3 ton market gardener's truck sold for £335.

During the Second World War many thousands of these Ford 10 cwt vans were in use as mobile canteens serving the armed forces and civilians. A great number were donated and run by voluntary services.

A wartime Ford chassis with horsebox body.

Towards the end of the Second World War some 2 ton chassis were available, identified by the wire mesh radiator grille.

18

Fowler

John Fowler & Company (Leeds) Ltd was registered in 1886 and manufactured steam traction engines. Fowler built steam-powered lorries from 1924 until 1935 and during this time a total of 117 were constructed, but they were not entirely successful due to steaming problems. The exception was the Fowler gulley emptiers, which latterly formed a large part of Fowler's production, so it would seem that providing frequent stops were made, steam pressure could be maintained.

In 1931 Fowler introduced its first diesel-engined lorry, which was a semi-forward control model for 6/7 ton payloads. This, and the following six-wheeled 10–12 ton vehicle, had a massive frontal appearance, but they do not appear to have proved popular with the road haulage industry. The company lilted both models with its own oil engine of six-cylinders, of 4⅜in diameter by 7in stroke, with the pistons having a patented cavity.

Fowler ceased production of goods vehicles in 1935, concentrating on a range of agricultural tractors and machinery which had been manufactured since approximately 1910.

A 1931 Fowler 6/7 ton heavy-oil engined lorry and trailer.

A typical Fowler with a heavy load. Does it look like an over-fat Boxer dog?

19

Garner

Henry Garner Ltd started in 1909, when the name was changed from Moseley Motor Works, which had commenced two years earlier. Production was spasmodic to say the least, but fortunes changed in 1927 when the name was changed to Garner Motors Ltd.

A large range was produced, although the sales figures may not have been very high. The most popular vehicle appears to have been the model 4JO, introduced in 1931, for a 4 ton payload. This was powered by a 22.4 hp four-cylinder petrol engine, with a choice of four wheelbases.

In 1933 Garner was merged with Sentinel and the 4JO model was produced at the Shrewsbury works until 1936. A very modern-looking vehicle was produced with a radiator grille which was similar to that used by Sentinel itself when it commenced production of its own diesel lorries in 1946. Just prior to the Second World War in 1939, the firm made some Garner-Straussler specialist military vehicles which were fitted with twin Ford V8 engines.

A 2½ ton chassis with a 13ft 8in wheelbase with a van body of 1,030 cu ft capacity and an interior length of 17ft by 8ft height.

A 1932 2 ton Garner model AB dropside lorry. The wheelbase is 11ft long and the body length is 10ft 4in by 6ft 6in wide with 16in sides.

The model JO6 was a 4 ton chassis with a 12ft 5in wheelbase. The body could carry a mixed load of 10, 12 or 17 gal milk churns – hence the upper deck on the front part for carrying the 10 gal churns. A six-cylinder 36 hp engine was fitted.

A six-wheeled model TW60s mobile public address van which had a six-cylinder 56.6 hp engine and a 4 ton load capacity.

20

Garrett

Richard Garrett & Co Ltd had its headquarters at Leiston in the heart of the Suffolk farmland, and therefore it is not surprising that production centred on agricultural machinery and traction engines, for which the firm was well known and respected. Among its successes in this field must be mentioned the Suffolk Punch tractor.

The first Garrett steam lorry was produced in 1904 and the company entered the field of battery-electric vehicles in 1921, also making some trolleybuses in 1928. The first Garrett diesel engined lorry appeared in 1930, fitted with a Blackstone six-cylinder engine.

During the 1930s the company became part of the Beyer Peacock Group and the production of road vehicles was slowly phased out so that by 1939 the works were making other engineering products.

Left: A beautifully restored Garrett six-wheeled steam wagon, few examples of which now exist. (R. G. Pratt)

Below: The first diesel lorry built by Garrett was in fact a steam wagon with a diesel engine and radiator placed in the front of the chassis.

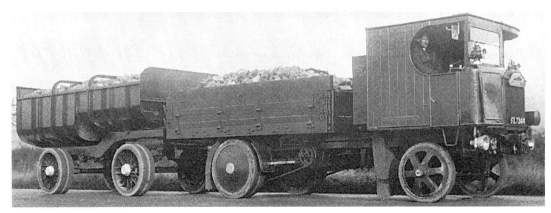

21

Gilford

The Gilford Motor Co Ltd of High Wycombe started off as E. B. Horne & Company of Holloway Road, London N7 in 1926 when it was converting war surplus vehicles. Just over a year later the company moved to larger premises at Bellfields, High Wycombe, where it began to produce a range of buses and coaches, which were popular with their operators, and many saw a long life. The petrol engines were originally of USA design and incorporated many components imported from that country; in fact the Gilford used many components from other manufacturers. The chassis was noted for the lilting of Grass auxiliary air springs to the front suspension which assisted comfortable riding qualities.

The range of Gilford goods vehicles was not so large, nor so popular, as the buses and coaches, and experiments with the four-wheel drive system with the introduction of the Tangye oil engine were almost a disaster, certainly in the early stages.

The AS6 model, for small passenger vehicles, was used for goods vehicles from 1930–1936, also the DF6 model. It had a six-cylinder petrol engine of 31.5 hp and a low underslung rear axle. Vacuum servo assisted rear wheel brakes were fitted. One of this type has been preserved, in fact it is the only known Gilford goods vehicle now in existence. The company went out of business in 1937.

A 1930 Gilford SF6 model 2½/3 ton lorry powered by a six-cylinder 85 hp engine.

A 1931 model AS6 van originally owned by Danish Bacon Co and now preserved. The chassis was normally used for twenty-seat coaches, but in this case it carried a 50 cwt payload.

22

Guy

Guy Motors Ltd was formed in 1914 at Fallings Park, Wolverhampton by Sydney S. Guy, following his resignation as Works Manager for Sunbeam Motor Car Co Ltd. The first vehicle to be produced was a 30 cwt lorry, with a then revolutionary device – now called an overdrive! The First World War intervened with the production of other vehicles until 1920, when a farmer's lorry was produced fitted with 'spud' wheels for traversing muddy ground. An articulated lorry followed in 1922, a battery-electric refuse collector a year later, and then followed a variety of vehicles, all of normal control.

The turning point for Guy commercial vehicles came with the introduction in 1933 of the Wolf, normal control 2 ton model. The Vixen 3/4 ton followed and a year later Guy had another triumph with the Otter 6 ton chassis, which weighed under 2½ tons fully equipped.

It was in 1934 that the famous radiator cap with the Red Indian head and the slogan 'Feathers in our Cap' first appeared, which was to be the company's symbol until its demise.

Civilian vehicle production ceased in 1938 as Guy took up urgent government contracts for military vehicles, which continued throughout the war. A variety of military material was manufactured, including on the vehicle side the six-wheeled lorries, the well-known Quad-Ant gun tractors, and even a light tank. However, in 1941 the company were allowed to produce some vehicles for hauliers with special MoWT licences. These were the Vix-ant, a basic Vixen with many Guy Ant (a military 15 cwt) parts, including the bonnet and radiator, which were of distinctive, and certainly 'utility' appearance.

A 1922 Guy model J 25 cwt truck powered by a 17 hp engine and now preserved, having delivered coal for twenty-nine years.

Two 1932 Guy 30/40 cwt model UVU vans. Incidentally this operator had a fleet of twenty-three Guy vehicles – so they kept them running!

A 1936 J type lorry.

A 1935 Guy Wolf 2 ton van with four-cylinder (90mm by 13mm) 50 hp engine. The wheelbase is 10ft 6in and the overall length is 16ft ½in, the body length being 9ft 6in.

This Otter 6½ ton lorry was supplied in 1939.

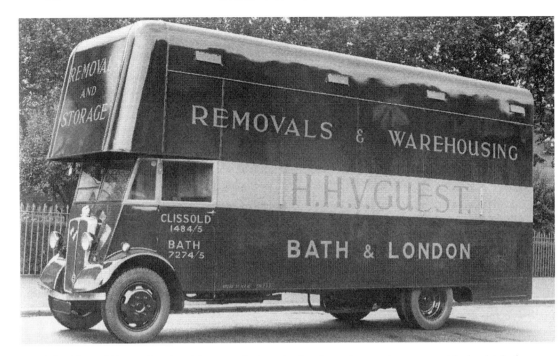

The Vixen 3/4 ton chassis with pantechnicon body of maximum size was an ideal vehicle for removal and storage work.

The 1940-dated Wolf normal and forward control Vixen side by side.

23

Halley

Halley Industrial Motors, which started as the Glasgow Motor Lorry Co, was first registered in 1906, producing both steam and petrol driven vehicles. The company won both gold and silver awards with their two-cylinder, 30 cwt and 2 ton models in the 1907 trials which lasted for seventeen days. The early engines were made by Tylor, but from 1910 Halley began making its own 25 hp and 35 hp four-cylinder engines, plus a large six-cylinder unit which developed 50 bhp.

The pre-1914 output was considerable and Halley was considered to be among the big ten motor vehicle manufacturers. The firm were particularly successful with the manufacture of fire appliances, which were in use by many Scottish brigades.

From 1914–18, Halley made shells and only a few vehicles were produced. When peace returned the company produced its new P series 3½ ton (or 29/35 seat) chassis with a six-cylinder engine. At first this proved to be a good seller, but the depression of the period had its effect and sales began to slump. A 2 ton S model was also produced, but this never sold in great numbers.

The early vehicles had a radiator with a shape similar to those on the Associated Daimler vehicles of c. 1926, but with the name Halley cast in the header tank. Later models had a pointed radiator.

In 1927 the company went into liquidation and re-emerged with the name changed to Halley Motors Ltd. Unfortunately, sales slowly declined yet again, and production ceased in 1935, when the firm finally closed and the works at Yoker were acquired by Albion, who used the premises as a packing plant for CKD export models, and also as a servicing plant.

A 2½ ton Halley van of 1929 which is now preserved and seen here on the HCVS London–Brighton run in 1969. (S. W. Stevens-Stratten)

A 2 ton tipping lorry of 1930.

24

Hallford

Hallford vehicles were produced from 1906 by the well-known and long established firm of J. & E. Hall, of Dartford, Kent, the name being a corruption of Hall and Dartford. The firm produced a 25 hp four-cylinder engine using Saurer patents, and early success came in 1907 in the RAC Commercial Motor Trials when a 3 ton lorry was awarded a gold medal plus a special diploma. Hallford then used its own design of engine in a range of vehicles from 35 cwt to 5 ton.

In its early days, the company undertook many experiments with petrol-electric traction for Thomas Tilling, which were later incorporated into the Tilling-Stevens vehicles built at Maidstone. A large number of these were buses, but a few commercials were produced under the Hallford banner. Hallford continued some vehicle production under its own name, and during the First World War was responsible for the manufacture of a large number of chassis for army lorries, of conventional design for the period.

After the war, the firm closed its motor manufacturing activities in 1923, rather than use capital for costly new designs and development in a competitive market, where its present models were outdated. Hallford products were distinguished by a bonnet top which sloped down to a pointed radiator top.

The Hallford 1914 WD type 3 tonner, now restored and seen at the first HCVC rally in 1958 at the Spurrier works, Leyland.

25

Karrier

Clayton & Company of Huddersfield started Karrier Motors Ltd in 1904, although the name was not used until 1920. The first range of vehicles was designated, sensibly, the A-type, which had the driver sitting in a high position above the engine. Payloads from 2 tons to 5½ tons could be supplied, all with Tylor engines of various sizes. Chain drive was standard, as were cone clutches.

One of the first vehicles of the newly-named company was the K-type; this was a normal control vehicle of which there were five models in the range, which was produced until 1931. The H-type was a four-wheeler for 2 ton payloads with either normal or forward control configuration, which was introduced in 1923 and remained in production until the early 1930s; the GH4 being a variation for 4 ton payloads. In 1929 the ZA model proved popular as it was a small normal control chassis for a 25 cwt load.

One of Karrier's many contributions to the industry was the development work it undertook in conjunction with the London Midland & Scottish Railway for a replacement of the horse and the Karrier Cob three-wheeled tractor was the result. This was introduced in 1931 and continued in production until 1938, being powered by a Jowett 7 hp engine.

The Karrier Motor Company was taken over by the Rootes Group in 1934 when production was moved from Huddersfield to Luton being allied to the Commer concern, which by then was also under Rootes control.

The CK range, introduced in 1935, proved very successful and some models continued in production until 1952. Another prewar success was the Bantam, a forward control, small wheeled, vehicle for 2/3 ton loads, often being used as the chassis for refuse collectors and other municipal vehicles, as well as a short-wheelbase version being extensively used as the motive power for semi-trailers. This again continued in production after the war, albeit with a modernised frontal appearance. During the Second World War Karrier produced army lorries, and other munitions work.

Two Karrier 3½ ton Victor models of 1932 fitted with lightweight bodies and powered by a four-cylinder (95 mm by 140 mm) 47 hp engine.

In 1933 this 50 cwt lorry with a Dorman-Ricardo heavy oil engine is undergoing a test run near Calver.

One of the early Bantam 2 tonners of 1934. This tipping lorry had a four-cylinder (69 mm by 90 mm) 11.8 hp engine.

One of the successful CK3 models. This 15 cu yd van was fitted with a moving floor.

Another CK3, on motorised refuse collection in 1936.

The Bantam 2 tonner was popular with many operators and used to carry a variety of loads. Here is part of a fleet of a well-known goods and parcels carrier.

One of the very early Karrier Cob mechanical horses in 1931.

A Karrier Colt three-wheeler for light loads. Manoeuvring in congested areas was easy. This photograph was taken in 1933.

Above and below: One of the original and primary ideas for the introduction of the mechanical horse – complete compatibility for trailer haulage by horse or mechanical transport.

26

Lacre

When the company was founded in 1902 in Long Acre, in the Covent Garden area of London, the thoroughfare was known as the street of car dealers. Lacre was a contraction of Long Acre.

The firm produced cars and its 25 cwt, 16 hp van appeared in 1904 after which Lacre continued with the production of small vans, achieving considerable success with sales to London retail stores.

In 1910 the company commenced production of commercial vehicles at a new factory in Letchworth, Hertfordshire, where a range extending from 10 cwt to 10 ton payload was made. Some of the larger vehicles saw service in France during the First World War.

The model 'O' was introduced in 1909 which was a highly successful normal control 2/2½ ton payload chassis with a wheelbase of 12ft fitted with a four-cylinder engine developing 30 hp. A three-speed gearbox coupled to a cone clutch and a double chain-driven rear axle was also standard.

By being updated, the basic 'O' model continued in production until 1935.

A 30/35 cwt model appeared in 1921 with a wheelbase of 10ft 6in and in the same year the larger model was given the option of a 38 hp engine. In 1922 a 4 tonner was produced known as the Colonial type or 'N' model.

The firm also made its name with the design and production of three-wheel roadsweepers, the single wheel at the rear being chain-driven from a Dorman petrol engine of 11.8 hp. Production of these strange looking machines started in 1919 and finished in 1936.

Due to financial difficulties the original company was wound up in 1928, but was reconstituted immediately with the title changed to Lacre Lorries Ltd, establishing new works at Welwyn Garden City. It is worth recalling that the designer for Lacre Lorries was J. S. Drewry – see under Shelvoke & Drewry.

A 1913 Lacre model O 2 ton van, which saw service in the First World War has been faithfully restored and preserved. Seen here on the 1972 HCVS Brighton Run. (S. W. Stevens-Stratten)

27

Latil

Latil was a French vehicle manufacturer established since 1904, whose products were originally marketed under the name Blum-Latil. Latil Industrial Vehicles Ltd was formed in the UK in 1924, but from 1932 vehicles were produced under licence by Shelvoke & Drewry. Latil products were then given the subsidiary name of Traulier. Most of the production consisted of four-wheel drive tractors, with an auxiliary gearbox. Latil's own petrol engine was originally fitted, but in later years alternative power units were available, usually a Meadows diesel. It would appear that one of the drawbacks of the Latil was the large turning circle required to undertake a 360° turn.

Latil made several tractors for railway shunting, utilising four small flanged steel wheels which acted as guides on the railway track, the power coming from the normal road wheels which rested on the rail surface, for the front and rear track of Latil tractors was the same as the standard railway gauge.

A forestry tractor supplied in 1935 and exhibited at the Royal Agricultural Show in Bristol the following year. Fitted with a winch, the stakes on the wheels could be folded down for extra grip on muddy ground. It had a four-cylinder petrol engine of 20.1 hp (RAC rating).

One of the experiments of the Shelvoke & Drewry regime was the adaptation of this Traulier tractor for road/rail use in 1936. As the track of the vehicle was the same as the railway gauge (4ft 8½in) the small steel wheels could be lowered to act as guides.

28

Leyland

Leyland Motors Ltd, which for the period covered by this book was one of the largest commercial vehicle manufacturers, began its existence as the Lancashire Steam Motor Company in 1896, building steam wagons, its first being a 30 cwt, fitted with a 10–14 hp two-cylinder compound engine, fed from an oil-fired boiler. This was followed by a more conventional 3 tonner and thus they progressed, so that by 1904 the company had produced seventy-two steam lorries or buses. Steam-powered vehicles were taken out of the Leyland sales literature in 1926. The first experimental petrol engined lorry was made in 1904, but it was not a success; however a year later the company was producing petrol buses for London as well as some lorries.

In 1907 the name was changed to Leyland Motors Limited and a range of heavy vehicles (nothing under 3½ tons) was now offered with either steam or petrol propulsion. Success came with the introduction of the 3 ton lorry which became known as the RAF type, as during the First World War nearly 6,000 were produced, the model being continued until 1926. Many different models were produced during the 1920s.

The year 1929 saw Leyland with a completely new range, all given names of animals – Badger, Buffalo, Bison, Bull, etc., which became almost household words in the commercial transport field.

In 1931 the Cub made its appearance, a highly successful 2 tonner built at the works at Kingston-upon-Thames. This lightweight was fitted with a six-cylinder engine and had hydraulic brakes acting on all four wheels.

In 1933 Leyland was able to offer an oil engine as an alternative to the petrol engine for its range and the former soon became popular as a more economic unit.

Leyland also offered several fire appliances, having an agreement with Metz, the German turntable ladder manufacturers, and with Dennis were the major builders of fire appliances prior to the Second World War.

During the hostilities, Leyland was fully occupied, manufacturing the Convanter tank, engines for the Matilda tank, assembling Churchill tanks and also producing high explosive and incendiary bombs (over 11 million of these) and 20 mm shells. Some utility bus chassis and a few 10 ton Hippo lorries were also produced.

A Leyland steamer of c. 1905 alongside a model X of 1908. Both vehicles are now preserved.

A close-up view of the steam lorry shown above. (Stevens-Stratten Collection)

A Leyland of c. 1921 which was still in service twenty-seven years later.

The P type 6 tonner of 1920s was an early form of forward control with the driver perched high above the engine.

One of the early Cub models of 1931.

A Terrier six-wheeler of 1933 used on trunk work. This was also the name given to an Army type six-wheeler during the war.

A Leyland Badger TA4 of 1932, for a 4 ton payload.

A forward control Badger 5 tonner of 1934.

This 1935 Beaver
TC10 6 ton chassis has
an ebonite lined tank
body for the carrying
of hydrochloric acid.
A 32.4 hp diesel engine
is fitted.

A Hippo six-wheeler of
1936.

The Lynx 5/6 ton
four-wheeler was
introduced in 1937.
A six-cylinder petrol or oil
engine could be fitted.

McCurd

W. A. McCurd was an automobile engineer, who is believed to have been a 'one-man business' until 1913, when a limited company was formed and commercial vehicles were produced in premises at Slough, Bucks until 1927.

In 1912 a large 5 ton chassis was produced and was made until 1914, with a four-cylinder engine of 32.4 hp, the normal four-speed crash gearbox and cone clutch. Unusually at this time, a choice of worm or bevel drive was available for the rear axle.

One example is preserved.

Believed to be the only survivor, this 1913 McCurd van is being prepared for the start of an HCVS event. (Stevens-Stratten Collection)

Maudslay

The origins of the Maudslay concern go back to 1833 when Maudslay & Field became an engineering partnership and achieved some fame by improving a Gurney steam vehicle. The Maudslay family name became well known in many fields of engineering and the Maudslay Motor Company was formed in 1903 to manufacture cars and light vans. In 1907 a 3 ton lorry was produced, with a 30/40 hp four-cylinder engine, which won a gold medal in a RAC Industrial Motor Trial. In 1912 a range of 30 cwt, 3 ton and 5 ton chassis were produced. From 1914–18 some vehicles were made, but Maudslay concentrated mainly on parts for aero engines.

At the 1921 Motor Show a 3/4 ton, 4/5 ton, 5/6 ton and 6/7 ton with a 50 hp engine were on display.

However, the manufacture of buses and coaches became a primary function in the 1920s and 1930s, but in 1929 a 10 ton six-wheeled commercial vehicle chassis with a four-cylinder engine, rated at 75 hp, was produced. This appears to have saved a somewhat ailing company, and in 1933 the Mogul (Mk I) four-wheeled, 6 ton lorry, but rated in the 4 ton taxation class, was built. This was lilted with a Gardner engine.

The financial slump finally hit Maudslay, but in 1939 a completely new range of vehicles, designed by Siegfried Sperling (an Austrian who had recently left his home country) and fitted with Gardner engines, had been produced for the Commercial Motor Show of that year, which unfortunately had to be cancelled due to the Second World War. This new range appeared after the war and was successful.

During the war, Maudslay produced the Mogul and Militant two-axle vehicles plus much military equipment, opening a 'shadow' factory at Alcester, and undertaking much subcontracted work.

Opposite above: A 10 tonner of 1931 with a trailing rear axle.

Opposite below: A similar vehicle to that on the previous page, with a van body, which gives some idea of the amount of goods which could be carried.

The new Mogul introduced in 1938 for 7½ ton payloads had the option of a four-cylinder petrol or diesel engine.

Two earlier Mogul models of 1939. One wonders how Hurst & Payne allocated their fleet numbers!

The Merlin II was a 6 ton vehicle introduced in 1940 with a wheelbase of 11ft 6in and supplied with a four-cylinder petrol engine.

Another Merlin with platform body of 15ft length supplied in 1939.

This Mogul 7 tonner was delivered in 1940 for essential civilian use.

Morris Commercial

William Morris, later Lord Nuffield, had been producing cars for many years and some light vans had been built on car chassis from 1913, but it was not until 1924 that his company entered into the commercial vehicle market.

The first vehicle to have the Morris Commercial badge was a 1 ton lorry which with small updates, lasted in production until 1939. It was designated the 'T' model, with a wheelbase of 10ft 2in powered by a 13.9 hp side-valve engine as used in one of the car range. Then followed the 'L' type for 8 cwt payloads, but this was soon increased to 10 cwt, then 12 cwt and finally 15 cwt as the L2 model in 1930. An 11.9 hp engine was first used, but this was succeeded by the trusted 13.9 hp engine in the L2 model.

The 'D' type of 1927 heralded the entry of Morris into the six-wheeled field for 30 cwt and 2 ton loads. At one time Morris could claim to be the largest producer of six-wheeled chassis, and their use by the army was soon firmly established.

Taking over the old Wolseley Works at Adderlcy Park, Birmingham in 1933, Morris introduced a range of heavier vehicles, starting with the 'P' type or Leader 2½ tonner (soon uprated to 3 ton) with a 22.4 hp petrol engine.

The 'C' type was a new design for 1934 with semi-forward or normal control, while the Leader had the new design of cab and was again re-rated for 3/4 ton. The 'C' range was very popular and sold well in all its variants. This applied also to the 'CV' range introduced from 1937, which was also known as Equiload, distinguished by its vee-shaped radiator front.

Morris also produced bus chassis and provided some fire appliances. The company's sales to the Post Office and large companies made most commercial vehicle manufacturers envious, and, perhaps, justified their slogan 'British to the Backbone'. During the Second World War Morris produced large numbers of vehicles for the Armed Forces.

A 1927 van with electric lights and opening windscreen.

A demonstration 7 cu yd refuse collection vehicle.

With a specially treated body and chassis to resist the corrosive effects of salt, this six-wheeler with fully articulated rear axles was supplied to ICI in 1938.

The pleasing looks of the 1938 Equiload is well shown in this photograph of a 5 ton chassis with 1,500 gal petrol tank body by the Aluminium Plant & Vessel Co.

In 1938 the semi-forward control Equiload model was announced. This is the long wheelbase version.

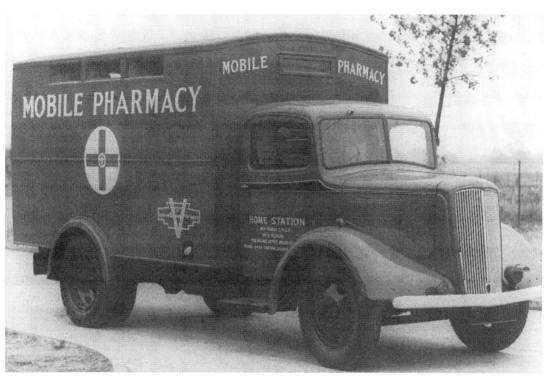

A wartime 3 ton van. Would you like to drive this in the blackout with these lights?

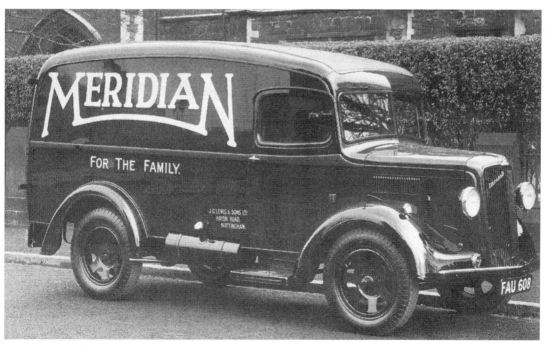

A Morris Equiload 25 cwt van of 1938 which again shows the clean lines and balanced look of the vehicle.

32

Pagefield

Pagefield was the name given to commercial road vehicles manufactured by Walker Brothers of Pagefield Iron Works, Wigan, Lancs, a firm which was formed in 1904, for general engineering, but produced a 2 ton lorry in 1907. By 1913 Walker Brothers was producing a subsidy 4 ton lorry using a 42 hp Dorman engine, and 519 were built for the services. Known as the N model it was produced, with some updates, until 1931. A 5 ton model, basically similar, was made in 1922.

In the mid-1920s and 1930s Pagefield became renowned for a unique refuse collecting scheme, whereby horse drawn trucks, with small diameter wheels, made the house-to-house collections, and when the trucks were full, they were winched up ramps on the back of a special Pagefield lorry and driven to the refuse tip. The lorry deposited an empty truck for the horse to continue the collection. Thus large towns needed only a few licensed lorries for this service.

In 1930 Pagefield produced some mobile cranes for the London Midland & Scottish and the London & North Eastern Railway companies using Dorman engines. Later, Tilling-Stevens petrol electric units supplied the power for transmission and lifting etc.

One of the company's popular models was the six-wheel, 12 ton Plantagenet chassis which was introduced in 1931 and powered by a Gardner 6LW diesel engine.

A similar 4 ton design on a four-wheel chassis was named the Pompian; there was also a 6 ton Pathfinder and Pegasix was the name given to a trailing axle six-wheeler. A 6/7 ton Paladin model followed and this range continued on a limited basis until the Second World War. During the war years, Pagefield made shells and sections for the Mulberry Harbour project, plus a number of special cranes.

A Pagefield Plantagenet six-wheel 12 ton lorry of 1932. A five-cylinder oil engine was fitted.

The Prodigy was introduced in 1932 for 3/3½ ton loads and from 1936 was available with a choice of petrol or diesel engine.

An example of the Pagefield refuse collection system. The trailer has been winched on to the lorry for the journey to the tip, but is drawn by a horse when making house-to-house collections.

A Pegasix supplied to J. Lyons in 1934 and powered by a Gardner 5LW diesel engine. The 6 ton payload could be increased by 4 tons if a trailer was hauled.

Peerless

This is not really a British company in the true sense of the word, for the vehicles in the UK were wartime imports from America and many thousands were used in France. After the First World War they were reconditioned by Slough Lorries & Components Ltd from whom, in 1920, a 5 ton lorry could be purchased for as little as £255. The company then became Peerless Trading Company and finally Peerless Lorries Ltd.

The Trader was a normal control lorry, built from available parts, but from 1925 was purpose built. All the parts were imported from the Peerless Motor Company of Cleveland, Ohio. Many of the vehicles had pneumatic tyres at the front, but solids on the rear; chain drive being used for the transmission.

Above: The Peerless Tradersix 90 with pneumatic tyres on the front and solids on the rear, allegedly giving better adhesion. Note the short drive chain to the rear axle.

Left: Another Tradersix. Note the hydraulic tipping arrangement.

Raleigh and Reliant

The Raleigh Cycle Company of Nottingham produced a three-wheeled light delivery van in 1930, which was designed by T. L. Williams and derived from the James Karryall. The first model, the LDV (Light Delivery Van) used a 598cc single-cylinder, side valve, air-cooled engine, and had a payload capacity of 5 cwt. The model was produced for three years when it was superseded by the Safety Seven for 8 cwt loads, fitted with a two-cylinder 742cc air-cooled engine, and the wheelbase was increased from 5ft 6in to 6ft 8in. Production ceased in 1935.

The Reliant Engineering Company of Tamworth produced the three-wheeled van, also designed by T. L. Williams, in 1936. This was a 7 cwt model with single-cylinder engine, but was soon followed by a two-cylinder, 10 cwt version. In 1939 a four-cylinder engine of 749cc was fitted to both 8 cwt and 10 cwt models which remained standard for many years.

A 1934 Raleigh three-wheeled 8 cwt van which is now preserved and seen on the HCVS London–Brighton Run in 1986. (S. W. Stevens-Stratten)

Scammell

The birth of Scammell vehicles goes back to a pioneering and experimental articulated lorry made in 1921 in Spitallields, London, when the idea of using a four-wheel tractor coupled to a two-wheeled semi-trailer became a reality. The advantage was a longer load space, plus greater payload capacity, which could be achieved without exceeding the legal axle weights.

The manufacturer of this innovation was G. Scammell & Nephewe Ltd, an old established firm of wheelwrights and coachbuilders. The experiment was successful so Scammell Lorries Ltd was formed a year later and moved to a factory at Tolpits Lane, Watford, where production began in earnest.

The original tractor units were chain-driven and many semi-trailer tankers were produced for carrying bulk liquids such as petrol and oil. The early tractive units were powered by 63 bhp four-cylinder side valve engines. In 1927 Scammell introduced the Pioneer six-wheeled tractor unit with a highly flexible suspension whereby there could be a 2ft vertical movement of each wheel and the chassis remained level.

In 1929 a four-wheel rigid vehicle was introduced for 6 ton payloads, and two years later a rigid-six which proved popular for 10 ton loads. Chain drive continued on the tractive units for some years to come.

Scammell was also famous for its three-wheeled tractive units – the mechanical horse – which was introduced in 1932. This vehicle was to revolutionise short haul collection and delivery services for the railway companies and for many municipal authorities for refuse collection. During the Second World War Scammell made many Pioneer tractors for tank recovery work, plus trailer pumps for the fire service.

Scammells have been used for articulated petrol tankers since the early days of the company. Here is a 1930 model.

The Rigid-Six of 1932 6x2 (meaning that only the first of the two rear axles is driven). From 1933 this could be offered with an oil engine as an alternative.

A c. 1921 chain-driven tractor and semi-trailer for the carriage of meat. (Courtesy Andrew Meadows)

A 1933 Scammell tanker.

One of the early Scammell Pioneers undergoing tests in 1932. This shows a good example of axle articulation at front and rear.

The rigid eight-wheeled 15/16 ton chassis was introduced in 1937 and remained available, virtually unchanged, until the arrival of the Routeman in 1960. The standard power unit was the Gardner 6LW diesel engine.

One of the two 100 tonners built in 1929 and 1931. Originally powered by the 80 bhp engine, they were subsequently converted to a Gardner 6LW. It is seen here traversing the level crossing at Warmley with a stator of Metropolitan-Vickers manufacture.

An early example of the Scammell mechanical horse.

A 6 ton mechanical horse in 1941.

Seddon

A relative newcomer to the commercial vehicle manufacturers, Foster & Seddon Ltd, of Salford, Lancashire, commenced production in 1937 with a 6 ton payload vehicle which weighed under 50 cwt unladen. For the previous eighteen years the firm had been engaged in the repair and maintenance side of the business.

This first production vehicle was a forward control, four wheeled, 6 tonner with a platform body and fitted with the standard Perkins P6 diesel engine, its six cylinders giving 65 bhp. A five speed gearbox, with overdrive on the fifth gear was standard. Some operators fitted an Eaton two-speed rear axle.

The vehicle had just proved itself as reliable and economic and was finding favour with customers when the Second World War broke out and production was halted. The story of its success belongs to the post-war period.

Above: Two Seddon 6 ton lorries awaiting delivery to a Bradford customer who used the same fleet number for both vehicles.

Left: Another Seddon 6 tonner for a Yorkshire brewery.

Sentinel

The name Sentinel is synonymous with steam wagons, which were acclaimed throughout the world. The Scottish firm of Alley & McLellan of Polmadie, Glasgow, established the Sentinel in 1906, and moved to Shrewsbury in 1918. The vehicles were highly successful and until crippling legislation and taxes hit the steam road vehicles, they could be seen in many spheres of road haulage, for they were efficient, reliable, modern and virtually silent. A testimony to this is the fact that as late as 1950 – well over a decade since the last Sentinel steamer had been built for the UK market, the firm received an order for 250 six-wheelers from the Argentinian Naval Authority.

In the late 1930s the Sentinel steamers were fitted with such luxuries as electric speedometer drive, automatic cylinder lubrication, self-stoking boilers (filled through the cab roof), a power take-off for a dynamo, a small compressor for a tyre pump, plus – if required – tipping gear and steam heaters for keeping loads hot – such as tar, etc.

The range of models was large and improvements were continually made over the years; a conventional prop shaft having succeeded chain-driven rear axles.

Sentinel also produced the High Speed Gas (HSG) producer plant, which they took over from Gilfords, but even with wartime petrol restrictions gas producer plant never became popular with operators. Sentinel also became interested in the internal combustion engine before the war.

A Super Sentinel 6/8 ton four-wheeled steam lorry of 1925.

A type DG/6 supplied to Dunstable Portland Cement in 1932.

Another six-wheeler of 1931.

This DG/6 model is fitted with 40in by 9in giant pneumatic tyres and carries a 12 ton payload.

The last steam design from Sentinel was the S6T model. This example is fitted with a three-way tipping body.

38

Shelvoke & Drewry

This firm was formed by a partnership of two ex-employees of the Lacre concern – Harry Shelvoke and J. S. Drewry – in 1923. Their initial production met with immediate success, for there was no competition for the ultra low loading vehicle they had designed. It was truly unique, with small 20in diameter wheels giving a 1ft 11in loading height, forward control with the driver sitting just ahead of the front axle, in a central position with tiller controls at either hand. The right hand tiller was for steering and the left for operating the vertically mounted epicyclic gearbox – three forward gears and one reverse.

The vehicles became popular with operators large and small, particularly with municipal authorities for use as refuse collecting vehicles where the low loading height was a considerable advantage. It was also economic in operation with a 14 hp engine, a top speed of around 15 mph, and also was highly manoeuvrable, with the added bonus that as the unladen weight was less than 2 tons it came into a low taxation class.

From 1932 to 1939, Shelvoke & Drewry also produced the Latil tractors, under licence from the French manufacturers. It must also be mentioned that Shelvoke & Drewry also produced a few special vehicles with normal steering just prior to the war.

This 1934 S&D was given by Epsom & Ewell Borough Council in 1965 to the Worthing & District Vintage Vehicle Society for preservation. It is interesting to note that Worthing operated a fleet of S&D Tramcars prior to the war. (S. W. Stevens-Stratten)

This vehicle was supplied in 1927 for petrol delivery.

A rear loading dustcart of 1932.

39

Singer

Nowadays, the name Singer is normally associated with sewing machines, but the Singer Motors Ltd of Birmingham produced a large range of motor cars over many years. From 1929–1932 Singer also manufactured a series of commercial vehicles for payloads of 25 cwt, 30 cwt, 2 ton and 45 cwt capacity.

Although they do not appear to have had vast sales, Singer lorries incorporated several novel features, including electric starting, which in those days was considered to be a great refinement.

The engine for the 2 ton model was a four-cylinder petrol unit of 3,053cc (90 mm bore by 120 mm stroke), which at 3,000 rpm developed over 57 bhp. The design of the overhead valve rockers reduced wear, while the lubrication system had no loose pipes. The chassis incorporated a Luvax foot-operated lubrication system supplying oil to the necessary parts, while the brakes were vacuum assisted. The engine was mounted on a three point suspension on a sub-frame insulated from the gearbox and clutch by rubber buffers. In the early 1930s this all added up to the most modern techniques.

The Singer Industrial Motors 2 ton lorry of 1930 with all 'mod con'.

A 25 cwt, six-cylinder, 160 cu ft capacity, van of 1931. Finished in bright red with black wings, wheels, lamps and bonnet, plus gold lettering, it must have looked most attractive

A 45 cwt chassis with a 500 gal petrol tank body in 1931.

Star

The Star Engineering Company was formed in 1904, having previously been the Star Cycle Company from 1896 when it took over the engineering concern of Sherratt & Lisle. The company's works were at Frederick Street, Wolverhampton, and were thus easy prey for a take-over by Guy Motors in 1927 who changed the name to Star Motor Company.

Early Star vehicles were based on a motor car chassis, but from the 1920s some goods chassis were produced for payloads from 15 cwt to 2 tons. A four-cylinder side valve engine of 3,054cc was fitted to the smaller vehicles, while an overhead valve engine was used for larger models.

The Star Flyer lived up to its name, being a fast vehicle with a six-cylinder, 23.8 hp engine, and carrying 3/4 tons. The wheelbase was 14ft 2in and the chassis was occasionally used for small passenger carrying vehicles.

The company continued as a separate entity under the Guy management until it went into liquidation in 1931.

An articulated tractor unit of 1931, based on the 50 cwt model with a 233.8 hp (RAC rated) engine. The semi-trailer was built by Dyson.

Two Bulldog 2 ton lorries supplied in 1932 to Blackpool Co-operative Society.

Thornycroft

The first Thornycroft vehicle was a steam van built in 1896 at Chiswick, which proved so successful that many steam wagons were built. In 1902 the first petrol engined Thornycroft vehicle appeared from the new works at Basingstoke.

One of the turning points in the company's history occurred in 1912 when it introduced the J type 4½ ton lorry powered by a 30 hp side valve engine. This vehicle became a subsidy type and over 5,000 were supplied to the government during the 1914–18 war. The J type continued in production, with a larger 50 hp engine until 1926.

The next success was in 1924 with the A1 chassis for 30 cwt loads, and this and a modified chassis coded A2 for 2 ton loads was the basis for a great variety of different bodies and many thousands were sold.

The PB forward control chassis came in 1928 and the QC six-wheeler in 1931 with a payload capacity of 12 tons. From 1933 all the Thornycroft range were given names rather than letters – the Handy being the successor for the A1/2 models.

In 1933 Thornycroft produced the Taurus 6 tonner with the engine placed ahead of the front axle, giving a snout effect, but allowing maximum load length for the given wheelbase. Another innovation around 1932 was the Stag six-wheeler using lightweight construction so that the unladen weight was under 7 tons for a 12 ton payload.

Other successful designs were the Sturdy for 6 ton payloads introduced in 1936 and the Nippy 3 tonner a year later, both these models being manufactured during the Second World War for essential civilian operation.

Thornycroft produced its first diesel engine in 1933 and thereafter these engines were available as an option for most of the range of models.

During the Second World War Thornycroft produced the Nubian four-wheel drive vehicle and Bren gun carriers. Thornycroft had considerable experience with cross-country vehicles, having supplied many pre-war army vehicles and others for the export market.

Above: A 1910 box van supplied to the Leeds Industrial Co-operative Society.

Left: A 1919 J type 4 ton lorry, the same as the 1913 subsidy type. This example has now been preserved. (Stevens-Stratten Collection)

One of the first Thornycroft vehicles to be fitted with an oil engine in 1931.

A Manly 2 ton lorry of 1934. The body length is 11ft.

Left: The Dandy 3 ton chassis is used for this 1,000 cu ft van.

Below: The Nippy 3 ton forward control chassis proved popular with many operators. This example has a 1,300 cu ft van body for a well-known removals firm.

Three Handy 2 ton forward control box vans supplied in 1934 to a well-known haulier.

The forward control Trusty 8 ton lorry in this photograph is used for retail coal and coke sales.

Just prior to the Second World War, Thornycroft announced its Sturdy 6 ton chassis, which became popular and was used by the armed services.

42

Trojan

Words used to describe the Trojan included 'weird', 'ugly', 'unique' and 'just plain horrible'! Yet this vehicle, designed by L. H. Hounsfield, was produced by Leyland Motors in its Kingston-upon-Thames factory from 1924 and at one time, production was at the rate of eighty-five per week. This association with Leyland lasted for four years, after which Trojan set up its own production plant at Purley Way, Croydon.

The original model, of 1924, carried a 5 cwt payload, had thin solid tyres, chain drive, a two-speed epicyclic gearbox, the footbrake operated on the rear wheels and the handbrake on the transmission. The engine was a unique four-cylinder, two-stroke rated at 10 hp (63.5 mm by 120 mm) and it had only seven moving parts!

Two years later a 7 cwt model was produced, which could be fitted with pneumatic tyres and this lasted until 1933 when an improved model capable of taking a 10 cwt load was introduced. It still used the same engine but the cylinders were now 63.5 mm by 117.5 mm. This model remained until 1937 when the 12 cwt Senior was announced and this was fitted with Bendix-Cowdray brakes, but all the other features remained. One of the largest users of Trojan vans was Brooke Bond Tea, but many small retailers found them economical and easy to maintain.

Brooke Bonds Tea was among the largest users of Trojan vans. Here is a 1930-type van. (Pamlin Prints)

This 1934 Lightweight 7/10 cwt van, featuring glass fibre reinforced plastics body panels has been preserved and is seen here on the HCVS Brighton run in 1965. (S. W. Stevens-Stratten)

43

Vulcan

The Vulcan Motor & Engineering Company Limited of Crossens, Southport, Lancashire, was founded in 1904, producing a small number of vehicles. The company had many financial problems during the 1920s and these continued in the early 1930s. The receiver was called in, for the third time, in 1936 but on this occasion the company was unable to recover and was purchased by the trailer manufacturer, J. Brockhouse who only wanted the works and the land. Tilling-Stevens therefore purchased the production rights and transferred the manufacture of Vulcan vehicles to its own works at Maidstone, Kent. At this time the range consisted of 2½ ton, 3 ton, and 5 ton chassis which were continued with the option of different engines including a Vulcan one manufactured since 1932.

Tilling-Stevens had designed a new 6 ton forward control model, known as the 6VF, which would have been introduced at the 1939 Commercial Motor Show, had it not been cancelled due to the Second World War. However, the company was able to produce this model for the civilian market from 1940 and with a choice of a petrol or diesel engine. Many operators took delivery of these vehicles as they were virtually the only new vehicles available. These vehicles produced in wartime austerity conditions had a wire mesh type of radiator grille.

A 1920 Vulcan model VSC 30 cwt lorry which has now been preserved.

A 1934 3 ton low loading refuse collector, fitted with hydraulic underslung tipping gear.

A 50 cwt van of 1930.

A 1938 model 5 ton lorry.

The Vulcan 6VF model introduced in 1939 which was in limited production during the war years.

44

Some Smaller British Manufacturers

Belsize

Belsize fire appliances were built in conjunction with John Morris & Sons Ltd of Salford, and it appears that joint marketing arrangements were made. One of the earliest models was made in 1912 and production ceased in 1921. This 1912 model, now preserved, has a six-cylinder 14 litre, 79 hp engine. The wheelbase is 11ft. A Morris Ajax 60ft wheeled escape is carried. The appliance was converted to pneumatic from solid tyres in the late 1920s. It was used by the Southampton Fire Brigade and seen here on the HCVS Brighton run in 1965. (S. W. Stevens-Stratten)

Crossley

Crossley Motors of Manchester was generally known as a bus builder, but in 1914 it made the RFC model ambulance and light van for the Royal Flying Corps. A Crossley four-cylinder engine of 4,531cc (101.6 mm by 140 mm) was fitted. The wheelbase is 11ft 4in long. This 1918-built restored van is participating in the HCVS London–Brighton run in 1974. (S. W. Stevens-Stratten)

Crossley produced a few goods chassis in the 1920s and 1930s and this is a 4/6 ton Beta model lorry of 1934 fitted with a four-cylinder 31.5 hp engine.

Tilling-Stevens

Tilling-Stevens of Maidstone was a pioneer in the petrol-electric system of transmission and generally concentrated on the passenger chassis market. However, several chassis were used for commercial or goods bodies and a few goods chassis were produced in the late 1920s and 1930s. Tilling-Stevens produced searchlight lorries for the army during the Second World War. This photograph shows a 4 ton van of 1931.

Walker

Battery electric propulsion began as early as 1905, and in the early 1920s several makers were experimenting with this form of power. However, it was not until the petrol rationing of the 1940s and early 1950s that battery electric vehicles really became a practical proposition for operators and manufacturers alike. This is a 1919 Walker 1 ton van (originally part American-built) which is now preserved. (S. W. Stevens-Stratten)

Yorkshire

The Yorkshire Patent Steam Wagon Co of Leeds had manufactured steam lorries from the early days of 1900 on a small scale. This 1914 6 ton steam wagon was new to the Colne Carrying Co. of Colne, Lancashire. It was later sold to Bilston Blast Furnaces and then to a brickworks near Uttoxeter. This 6 ton WE model is now preserved, and photographed at the Horsham Historic Vehicle Show in 1970. (S. W. Stevens-Stratten)